LET'S TALK ABOUT
NEEDING ATTENTION

D0521342

by Joy Berry • Illustrated by Maggie Smith

SCHOLASTIC INC.
New York Toronto London Auckland Sydney

ISBN 0-590-62424-5

12 11 10 9 8   9/9 0 1/0

Printed in Mexico.   24
First Scholastic printing, August 1996

Hello, my name is Peetie.

I live with Casey.

Sometimes Casey feels he needs more attention. Sometimes you might feel you need more attention, too.

You might feel you need attention because you are sick or hurt.

You might want someone to help you feel better.

You might feel you need attention because you are having a hard time doing something.

You might want someone to help you with what you are trying to do.

You might feel you need attention because you don't feel good about yourself.

You might want people to tell you that you are okay.

Or, you might want people to tell you that they like you.

You might feel you need attention because you are unhappy about a situation.

You might want someone to reassure you that things will be all right.

Or, you might want someone to help make the situation better.

You might try to get attention by
whining,
crying,
or throwing tantrums.

You might try to get attention by
complaining,
tattling,
or teasing.

You might try to get attention by
showing off,
interrupting,
or being rude.

You might try to get attention by disobeying.

Doing things that bother people will usually upset them.

Doing things that upset others will not get you the kind of attention you need or want.

There are more positive ways that you can get the help, encouragement, and love that you need.

Find a person who can give you some attention.

Tell that person exactly what you need or want.

Be polite when you ask for attention.

Try not to make demands or threats.

Try not to bother a person who is too busy to give you attention.

Instead, make a plan to spend time together when the person is not busy.

Then, patiently wait for that time.

People are more likely to give you attention if you give *them* attention.

So, it is good to give help, and encouragement, and love whenever you can.

Being patient and paying attention to others is the best way to get the attention you need or want.